DALE EARNHARDT

A LEGEND FOR THE AGES

TRIUMPH
BOOKS
CHICAGO

Author:
Bob Moore

Photography:
The Charlotte Observer

Editor:
Constance Holloway

Design Team:
Larry Preslar
Beth Epperly
Andrea Ross

This book is a joint production of
Triumph Books and the New Ventures
Division of Knight Publishing Co.

This book is available in quantity at
special discounts for your group or
organization. For further information,
contact:

Triumph Books
601 South LaSalle Street, Suite 500
Chicago, Illinois 60605
(312) 939-3330
Fax (312) 663-3557

Printed in the United States of America

ISBN 1-57243-550-X

Bob Moore has been covering NASCAR for 40 years, and he has
been around the sport even longer. His father raced during the late
1940s and early '50s. Moore began covering stock car racing in 1962
when he began his newspaper career at the Daytona Beach (Fla.) News-
Journal. He also worked for the Bradenton (Fla.) Herald and the Tampa
(Fla.) Times before moving to The Charlotte (N.C.) Observer in 1965.
Moore was The Observer's motorsports writer for just over 10 years.
Moore then joined Sports Marketing Enterprises, the sports-marketing
arm of R.J. Reynolds Tobacco Co., where he directed the public relations
section and its work with NASCAR for 15 years. In fall 1991, Moore left
SME to start his own motorsports marketing company. Since then, he has
co-authored two books, "The Thunder of America" and "NASCAR's 50
Greatest Drivers," and written for various publications including Area
Auto Racing News, FasTrack, Car and Driver, NASCAR Winston Cup
Scene and NASCAR Winston Cup Illustrated.

DALE EARNHARDT *Stats*

Cars:
Wrangler Jeans No. 3 Chevy (1st car) GM Goodwrench Service Plus No. 3 Chevy (2nd car)

Major Wins:
76 (Winston Cup)
- Six-time Busch Clash winner ('80, '86, '88, '91, '93, '95)
- Three-time winner of The Winston ('87, '90, '93)

Earnings:
$42 million

Poles:
22

Top 5 Finishes:
281

Top 10 Finishes:
428

Championships:
- Seven NASCAR Winston Cup championships ('80, '86, '87, '90, '91, '93, '94)
- Four-time IROC champion ('90, '95, '99, '00)
- Five-time NMPA Driver of the Year ('80, '86, '87, '90, '94)
- American Driver of the Year ('87, '94)

Teams:
Nine
- Owners — Ed Negre, W. Ballard, Johnny Ray, Henley Gray, W. Cronkite, Ron Osterlund (4 years), Jim Stacy, Bud Moore, Richard Childress (19 years)

Sponsors:
(Old ones —Wrangler Jeans, Miller, STP) GM Goodwrench Service Plus, Remington Arms, Coca-Cola, Snap-On Tools, Food-City and Chevrolet.

Fun Facts:
He diversified one step further in 2001 when he competed in the Rolex 24 At Daytona, driving a factory-prepared Chevrolet Corvette with Earnhardt Jr. Earnhardt has won nearly every major event and title available to NASCAR Winston Cup drivers, including the Daytona 500, Southern 500, Coca-Cola 600, etc. The only Winston driver to win rookie of the year and the championship in successive years (1979, 1980).

TABLE OF CONTENTS

Chapter 1
Fame Beyond the Track 6

Chapter 2
Following in Dad's Footsteps 12

Chapter 3
The Breakthrough Race 20

Chapter 4
Earnhardt's Greatest Victory 24

Chapter 5
Toughest Loss of All 30

Chapter 6
Racing Against Dad 34

Chapter 7
Another Kind of Horsepower . . . 36

Chapter 8
DEI: A Powerhouse Team 40

Chapter 9
If God Was a Stock Car Driver . . 44

FAME BEYOND *the track*

The first line of the story said it all — stock car racing will never be the same.

The death of Dale Earnhardt Sr. on the final lap of the 2001 Daytona 500 changed the face of the sport forever.

All you needed was one trip to a NASCAR Winston Cup race to realize the impact Earnhardt had on the sport. Everywhere you went there were Earnhardt hats and T-shirts and jackets and the black No. 3. And when he was introduced the noise was deafening as the cheers — and boos — seemed to go on for hours, not minutes.

As far as the fans were concerned, there was no middle ground. You either loved "The Intimidator" or you despised "The Man in Black."

And his fame went far beyond the race track. If you asked people in London or Tokyo or Moscow if they knew anything about stock car racing, like Richard Petty in the era before, the first name they would mention would be Dale Earnhardt. And if they knew nothing about the sport, his would be the only name that came across their lips.

Because of his humble beginnings ("When I came into Winston Cup, I didn't have nothing," he said on more than one occasion), the fans saw Earnhardt as one of them, but one who was able to fulfill his dream.

And then there was his ability behind the wheel of a race car. Just two days before his death in the IROC (International Race of Champions) race at Daytona International Raceway, Eddie Cheever knocked Earnhardt sideways as they battled for the lead with Earnhardt

Dale Earnhardt Sr. with Jeff Gordon

sliding into the grassy area. Somehow, Earnhardt was able to keep the car going in the right direction. Dale Jarrett called it the "greatest save" he had ever seen.

And of course there is the infamous "Pass in the Grass" in the 1987 running of The Winston, NASCAR's all-star race, that wasn't really a pass as once again Earnhardt kept his car going straight after being slammed in the back by an angry Bill Elliott. Earnhardt slid through the grass and never lost the lead. There was no pass, but everyone there will always remember that day.

Andy Petree witnessed up close just how good Earnhardt was after he took over for Kirk Shelmerdine as the crew chief on the black No. 3 in 1993.

"You can go back through my notes and Kirk's notes, too — a number of times we didn't have the best car, but Dale won," says Petree. "He just had a way of finding a way to the front of the pack."

Of course, one of the ways he got to the front earned him that nickname — The Intimidator. Earnhardt would, as they say in the trade, "put a bumper to you" in his quest to win.

"Most people saw him as intimidating," says Petree, "but really it was his level of confidence in himself. He had that confidence that nobody could beat him. His confidence level is what gave him that edge."

When Earnhardt was asked about the nickname, he would flash that sly, mischievous grin of his as he said, "If you intimidate another driver when you drive up beside him, and you can go into the corner before he does, you win.

"You've got to have and use every resource that you have to win."

And win he did. He finished his illustrious career with seven NASCAR Winston Cup championships, tying him with Petty for first in this most important of categories. He won 76 races, sixth on the all-time list.

His last win will have to rank as one of his greatest — if not his most amazing. As David Poole of The Charlotte (N.C.) Observer said following the unbelievable victory, "Nobody can do what Dale Earnhardt did to win the Winston 500 at Talladega Superspeedway (on Oct. 16, 2000). Not even Earnhardt. Nobody can

be 18th with five laps to go and then have to spend the final lap worrying about being passed to have a win taken away. Nobody can run up the middle of a three-wide pack of screaming race cars and draft his way from oblivion to victory lane. Nobody can do that. Yet it happened."

And then there was Earnhardt the businessman. Here again he had no equal. He won more than $41 million on the race track and more than five times that off the track.

"When I first started racing in 1979 as a rookie, I was just so enthused and intrigued by a situation that I have never been in," said Earnhardt when asked when he realized that he needed to be a businessman as well as a racer. "Then when I won again (the championship) in 1986, I realized what it's (the sport) all about, what it meant to me, who I was and where I was at."

During the sport's greatest growth — the 1990s, Earnhardt was the man pushing the sport up the mountain. His fame and success on and off the race track played the leading role as NASCAR Winston Cup racing became the "world's fastest-growing sport."

And then there was the other side of Dale Earnhardt. The one he didn't let many people see. The one that brought seed for destitute farmers or loaned an engine to John Andretti at a time when Andretti was trying to get his Winston Cup career started. The one that put Dale Earnhardt Chevrolet on the side of Ernie Irvan's race car so Irvan could get his career off the ground.

Earnhardt didn't like to talk about his charitable side or the times he fulfilled a sick child's dream.

Nor did he say much about his ability to solve many a problem in the garage area by going directly to NASCAR President Bill France Jr. to get the controversy resolved.

The sport of NASCAR Winston Cup racing continues to reign as the only sport on TV where the ratings are going up.

However, there is something missing. It doesn't have that same feel.

And that is because there is no longer a black No. 3 acting as The Intimidator.

following in DAD'S FOOTSTEPS

For Dale Earnhardt, there was never any doubt about what he wanted to do for a living.

From almost the moment that he understood what Dad did, Earnhardt spent every possible minute hanging around Ralph's race shop. And when Ralph won the 1956 NASCAR Late Model Sportsman championship, young Dale was hooked.

Even though he was only 5 at the time he told everyone who would listen that someday he, too, would be a champion.

Yet before he fulfilled that dream — some 24 years later, Earnhardt's will to do what Dad did was tested over and over and over again. There were countless times when he could have quit.

By the time he reached 21, he had been married twice — both unions failed. And more times than the local bank would care to admit, Earnhardt was late on his payments.

Even when Ralph died suddenly in September 1973, Earnhardt didn't pause in his drive to become a success on the race track. First, he talked his mother, Martha, into giving him Ralph's two race cars instead of selling them. And then he took those cars and went back racing on the dirt tracks of the Carolinas and the neighboring states.

By this stage of his career, Earnhardt was winning races on a fairly regular basis. And this led to Ed Negre giving him his first start on the NASCAR Winston Cup

l-r brothers Danny, Randy and Dale Earnhardt play on their father Ralph's racer when Dale was about 8 years old. Randy, front, is on a soap-box derby racer.

Series in the 1975 World 600 at Charlotte Motor Speedway (now called Lowe's Motor Speedway). Earnhardt started 33rd and finished 22nd, completing 355 of the 400 laps. He earned $2,425.

Earnhardt ran two Winston Cup races in 1976 and one in 1977. Then in 1978, at the urging of H.A. "Humpy" Wheeler, general manager of Charlotte Motor Speedway, Will Cronkite put Earnhardt behind the wheel of his No. 96 Ford. Willy T. Ribbs was originally scheduled to drive the car, but Ribbs never showed up for the two-day special test the track had scheduled. Ribbs was caught going the wrong way on a one-way street in downtown Charlotte. So Wheeler asked Cronkite to put Earnhardt in the car. It would be the break that Earnhardt needed.

Six weeks later, Earnhardt ran a strong seventh in the Firecracker 400 at Daytona International Speedway and caught the eye of Rod Osterlund.

The first race Earnhardt ran for Osterlund was the Late Model Sportsman event at CMS in October. Despite bouncing off a few walls, Earnhardt finished second.

A few days later, Dave Marcis told Osterlund he was leaving the team at the end of the season since he and team manager Roland Wlodyka didn't see eye-to-eye on how the team should be run. Osterlund said he would begin searching for an experienced driver to replace Marcis for the '79 season as he didn't think his young driver, Earnhardt, was ready for a full-time ride on the Winston Cup Series.

Osterlund had agreed to run two cars in the next-to-last race of the year at Atlanta International Raceway.

Earnhardt was determined to show everyone that he was ready to move up. And that he did as he made sure everyone kept their eyes on the driver in car No. 98 as Earnhardt ran up front all day and finished an impressive fourth.

After the race, Earnhardt said, "All I have to say is I hope they give me this ride next year for the entire season. I think I can be tough. If some people didn't know before, they know now I can drive a race car."

Osterlund smiled as he listened. He had been converted into a Dale Earnhardt

fan, and a week later named the 27-year-old as the team's full-time driver.

Driving the No. 2 Buick for Osterlund, Earnhardt beat out Harry Gant and Terry Labonte to win the 1979 rookie-of-the-year title. In doing so, Earnhardt became only the third first-year driver in NASCAR history to win a race. Earnhardt's first trip to victory lane on the Winston Cup circuit came on April 1 in the Southeastern 500 at Bristol (Tenn.) International Raceway.

In 27 starts that year, Earnhardt won four poles, and had 11 top fives and 17 top 10s. It was a dazzling start to what would become one of the greatest careers in the history of NASCAR.

A year later, Earnhardt became the first and still only driver to follow up a rookie-of-the-year title with a NASCAR Winston Cup championship as he edged three-time champion Cale Yarborough by 19 points. Earnhardt won five races in capturing his first title.

He had now achieved his goal of becoming a champion, but a few more roadblocks were thrown in his path before he was able to add to that championship total.

In June 1981, Osterlund shocked Earnhardt and sponsor Wrangler by selling the team to J.D. Stacy. This upset Earnhardt to the point that in August he started looking for another ride. With the help of Junior Johnson and the folks at R.J. Reynolds Tobacco Co., the series sponsor, Earnhardt got hooked up with Richard Childress.

Although the start was a little bumpy, this partnership was to become the most successful in the history of the sport.

Earnhardt finished the '81 season in the No. 3 Chevrolet owned by Childress, but at the end of the year Childress told his young driver that his team wasn't up to the standards that Earnhardt deserved. As a result, Earnhardt and Wrangler moved to the Bud Moore-owned team.

Earnhardt won one race in 1982 and two more in '83 for Moore before deciding to reunite with Childress.

Earnhardt was now back behind the wheel of the No. 3 Chevrolet, a number and nameplate he would make famous. Wrangler was the sponsor and the colors of the car were blue and yellow. It

was during his seven years with Wrangler that Earnhardt became known as "One Tough Customer."

Earnhardt's second championship and first with Childress came in 1986. But this title almost never happened as during the '85 campaign Childress had given his driver the chance to move elsewhere.

"We won four races and finished eighth in the points," recalls Childress. "But we had nine DNFs (did not finish). After blowing up at the second Pocono race, I told Dale I wouldn't hold him to his contract, which had another year, if he wanted to leave and that we were not giving him the equipment for a driver of his caliber. He said, 'Naw, we're in this together, and we'll fix it together.'

"That's when we really bonded with confidence in each other and the team," adds Childress. "That was a momentous decision in the young existence of RCR Enterprises and a pivotal point in our careers together.

"We really went on a tear — winning five races and the championship in '86 and then coming back and winning 11 races (a series-high) and the championship again in '87."

GM Goodwrench came on board as the team's sponsor in 1988 to establish the famed black No. 3.

And it was under this color that Earnhardt earned his greatest fame and his two greatest nicknames — The Intimidator and The Man in Black.

Between 1988 and his death on Feb. 18, 2001, Earnhardt won four more Winston Cup championships (1990-91, '93-'94) and 45 races to bring his total to a record-tying seven titles and 76 victories. His win total places him sixth on the all-time list. He was the first driver to ever win more than $40 million in his career.

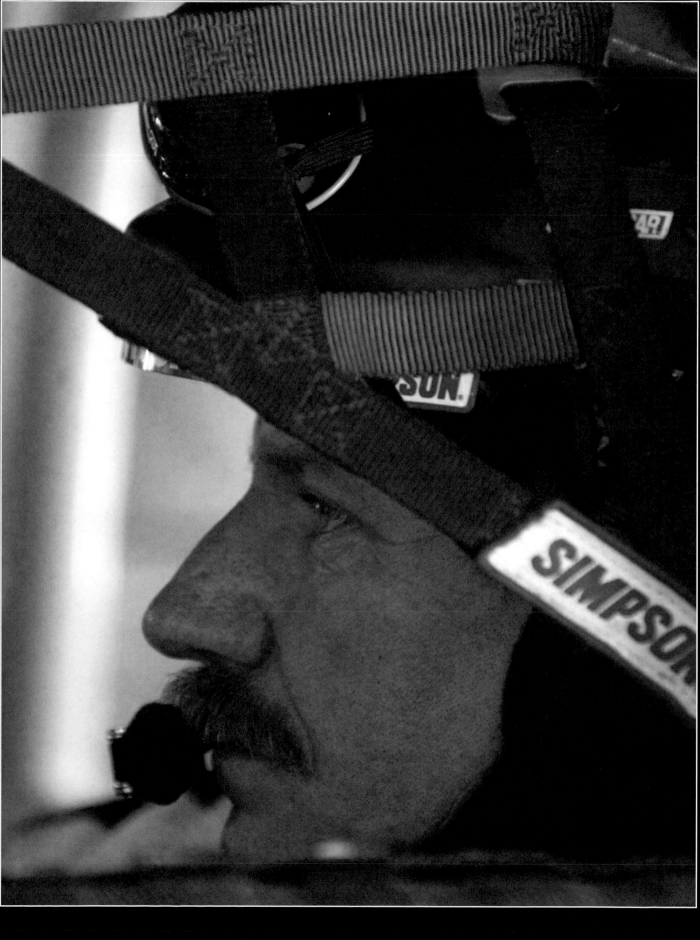

THE BREAKTHROUGH *race*

Second-year drivers are not supposed to contend for a NASCAR Winston Cup championship — even those who win the rookie-of-the-year title.

Yet as the 1980 season dwindled down to its final four races, none other than sophomore sensation Dale Earnhardt was leading the race for the point title.

And what made this even more surprising, Earnhardt was trying to hold off three-time champion Cale Yarborough, driving for the legendary Junior Johnson.

The racing experts kept waiting for Earnhardt and his young team, led by 20-year-old crew chief Doug Richert, to fold under the pressure.

However, even at this early stage of his Winston Cup career Earnhardt was displaying that grit and determination that

would be his standard-bearers throughout his race to the top of the success ladder.

And those attributes were never more on display than in the win that propelled him to the first of his seven championships, a victory that was made even more special because it came at his hometown track.

At the time, Earnhardt held a 105-point lead over Yarborough, and many people were telling him that he needed to change his driving style to a more conservative mode to ensure his place atop the point standings.

"I don't stroke," said Earnhardt. "I got here by running hard and I'll continue to do that."

And that is exactly what he did in the National 500 at Charlotte Motor

Dale Earnhardt admires the 1994 Observer Cup he was awarded at a NASCAR event.

Speedway (now Lowe's Motor Speedway) on that cool fall afternoon.

Earnhardt led a race-high 12 times for 143 laps in a highly competitive event that saw 43 lead changes among 11 drivers.

As the race entered its final 100 laps, it had turned into a three-driver affair among Earnhardt, Yarborough and pole-sitter Buddy Baker.

Earnhardt was the first of the trio to make his final pit stop on lap 280 of the 334-lap affair. His crew took only 13.1 sec-onds to give him two new right-side tires and fuel. Yarborough and Baker pitted four laps later with Yarborough's stop taking 17.1 seconds and 17.5 seconds for Baker.

Earnhardt's lead was now 5.3 seconds. Yarborough and Baker slowly began to cut into Earnhardt's lead, but the young driver from Kannapolis, N.C., never allowed them to get any closer than the 1.83 sec-onds that was the winning margin.

With Yarborough finishing second, Earnhardt padded his point lead to 115, a

big enough advantage that even with Yarborough winning two of the last three races, Earnhardt was able to secure his first championship. His winning margin was a mere 19 points.

In addition to being the win that lifted him to the title, the victory fulfilled a dream he had had since his father, Ralph, a Late Model Sportsman champion, had brought him to CMS as a young boy.

"No one can know how much I've dreamed and thought about this moment," said Earnhardt in victory lane following his National 500 win. Standing beside him was his mother, Martha, who was so overcome with emotion that she had trouble even congratulating her son.

"It's an even better feeling than I thought it would be. This is also where I got my (Winston Cup) start (driving for Ed Negre in 1975).

"I got a high when I won my first race at Bristol (during his rookie sea-son)," added Earnhardt. "I may not

show it, but I'm a lot higher now than I was then. This is the best, winning here at home before so many hometown family, friends and fans."

And it was a victory that, even years later as his win total surpassed the 50-win mark, Earnhardt would call one of the most important of his career.

"I don't know how you want to describe it, breakthrough or crucial or what, but that victory showed that we were a championship contender when so many people were expecting us to fold under the pressure," said Earnhardt. "The team gave me a great pit stop at a time when we needed it the worst. And we were able to go on and win the race and eventually the championship.

"And then it was my first one at Charlotte. It was a big win that came at a place where I really wanted to win. It was just a big win."

EARNHARDT'S
greatest victory

Dale Earnhardt holds up a sign for Dale Earnhardt Boulevard, which was renamed in his honor at Dale Earnhardt Day in Kannapolis.

For a man who won 76 races and seven NASCAR Winston Cup championships, one would think it would be extremely difficult to select one win that stands above the rest. But that is not the case with Dale Earnhardt.

And it came only a few days after being chosen as one of NASCAR's 50 greatest drivers.

For Earnhardt, his victory in the 1998 Daytona 500 was the win that he cherished the most.

"After coming so close so many times, finally winning it on my 20th try — and in NASCAR's 50th anniversary year — makes it extra special," said Earnhardt in victory lane.

Adds Richard Childress, "I know how important it was to Dale to have that

race on his record. He was Daytona's top winner (34 victories at the famed Daytona International Speedway), but we had lost or given away the Daytona 500 several times, a couple on the last lap."

Childress, owner of the famed black Chevrolet that Earnhardt drove, said he didn't "quit worrying that something bad was going to happen until Dale said on the radio, 'Boys, I can't believe we've won the Daytona 500, but we have.'

"I wanted to win it more for his sake than mine," added Childress.

And one could certainly understand why since Earnhardt's failure to win the biggest race of the season had become the story every year.

As Earnhardt himself noted a couple of days before winning the 500, "I get

asked all the time when I'm going to win at Daytona, and now folks are starting to ask me if I'll ever win the Daytona 500."

He paused before adding, to the surprise of no one, "Some of my biggest disappointments of my career have come in the Daytona 500."

Twice he had been leading when the white flag was waved. The first came in 1990 when a cut tire on the final lap enabled Derrike Cope to race past and score the surprising triumph. In 1993, Dale Jarrett was able to slip by just moments after the white flag was waved.

Three other times Earnhardt finished second — 1984, 1995, 1996.

And many people — not Earnhardt — forget how close he came to winning the race in 1986. "We had the fastest car that year," he would recall. "I was just sitting there behind (Geoff) Bodine waiting for the last lap. I had run him down and was just sitting there…" However, during his last pit stop, the crew hadn't got all the fuel in the car and Earnhardt ran out of gas with three laps to go.

"We have come so close so many times," noted Earnhardt. "If we keep running like we have here, we will win it. I have no doubts about that. Maybe it will be this year."

And finally it was.

After holding off a fast-closing Bobby Labonte to score the biggest victory of his illustrious career, Earnhardt said, "We've lost this race every way we could lose it. Now we've won it. Now we won't have to answer that question anymore."

The victory enabled Earnhardt to put an exclamation point on his unbelievable record at Daytona, a history that earned him the title of one of the most successful drivers in the history of Daytona International Speedway.

After all, he owned about every record that is available at the famed facili-ty including winning an unbelievable 10 straight Gatorade 125-mile qualifying races (1990-1999) and 12 overall.

He was the only driver to win three straight Budweiser Shootouts and his victory total of six is an event record.

Earnhardt also won a record four straight International Race of Champions (IROC) events at Daytona and six overall, another first.

In addition, Earnhardt won a record seven Busch Series races at the 2.5-mile superspeedway including a record — what else — three straight.

After finally winning the Daytona 500, Earnhardt and Childress celebrated that evening with champagne and cigars.

Childress laughs as he points out, "Even Dale, who hates cigars, took a few puffs. So I saw him do two things that day that I had not seen before.

"I didn't want to leave Daytona that night. It was that special of a day."

GM
Goodwrench Service Plus
GM
Goodwrench Service Plus
BURGER KING
Snap-on

What a lot of people don't remember about that day was the concern that the race was going to be rained out for the first time in the history of the 500.

And that was why the start of the 500 was moved up 10 minutes — in hopes of at least getting in 250 miles to make it an official race.

What really worried NASCAR President Bill France Jr. was the long-range weather forecast that said once the rain got to Daytona Beach it was supposed to linger for two or three days. Running the 500 on Wednesday was not something France or anyone else wanted.

Earnhardt took the lead for the first time on lap 17 and led 34 of the first 100 laps. And after swapping the top spot with pole-sitter Labonte, Jeff Gordon, Rusty Wallace and Childress Racing team-mate Mike Skinner, Earnhardt moved in front to stay on lap 140.

And despite repeated charges by a number of drivers during the final 60 laps, Earnhardt refused to relinquish his hold on the No. 1 spot.

"I was just working the mirror," said Earnhardt later. "I was working to keep the race car in front until somebody turned us over or we crossed the finish line first … nobody turned us over."

The race actually finished under the yellow flag as John Andretti and Lake Speed collided on the white-flag lap with both cars spinning down the backstretch.

"The Daytona 500 tops them all," said Earnhardt during the post-race interview in the press box. "It tops all the last 30 races I've won here. It tops them all. It puts the icing on the cake."

TOUGHEST
loss of all

For many years, the first thing you would see when you walked into the main race shop at Richard Childress Racing was a flat tire and wheel mounted over the door.

Even though the tire had been polished to a high sheen and attached to an expensive piece of wood, it was still quite a startling memento.

And naturally, there is quite a story behind it — one without a happy ending — for that is the tire that played the major role in the toughest loss of Dale Earnhardt's career.

The story actually begins in 1979 when Earnhardt made his debut in the Daytona 500. From that moment on, Earnhardt was a master at getting around the high-speed, 2.5-mile superspeedway.

In his first 500, he led five times for 10 laps and finished eighth. A year later, Earnhardt won the second running of the Busch Clash — now known the Budweiser Shootout, and he finished fourth in the 500 after leading seven times for 10 laps.

His second victory at Daytona came in the 1982 Goody's 300.

In 1986, he won the Busch Clash, one of twin Gatorade 125-mile qualifying races and another Goody's 300. However, Earnhardt wasn't able to make it a clean sweep as bad luck struck in the 500.

After his sensational week, Earnhardt began the 500 with high, high hopes. And as the race entered its final 50 laps, he was still feeling that way. Geoff Bodine

Kannapolis is trying to position itself as the place to go to learn about Dale Earnhardt. Fans can purchase memorabilia at Cannon Village.

was the leader, but Earnhardt was only inches off his rear bumper. Time and again, Earnhardt would move his car back and forth, messing with Bodine's psyche by making his car loose.

Bodine made his final pit stop of the day on lap 159 for fuel and right-side tires. His stop took only 15.2 seconds. A lap later, Earnhardt pitted. However, the stop did not go smoothly as the gas man failed to get all the fuel in and Earnhardt briefly stalled the car. As a result, Earnhardt was almost five seconds back of Bodine by the time he returned to the track.

But with drafting help from Benny Parsons, Earnhardt quickly ran down Bodine and pulled up to his rear bumper with still 24 laps to go. Instead of racing past his rival as many expected, including Bodine, Earnhardt elected to "sit there, just saving tires and gas.

"I was gonna race him on the last lap. I was where I wanted to be."

However, with three laps remaining, Earnhardt suddenly slowed. He was out of gas. Earnhardt slid past his pits with a dead engine. After pushing the car back into its pit stall, the crew put enough gas in to get the car restarted. But the engine was no longer performing at peak efficiency and Earnhardt limped home in 14th place.

A pattern had began to develop, a pattern that would become the headache of headaches for Earnhardt — he would dominate the races leading up to the Daytona 500 and run extremely well in the 500, but he was unable to win the race every stock car driver puts at the top of his wish list.

Earnhardt led the 500 again in 1987, '88 and '89 as he finished fifth, 10th and third respectively.

By the end of the decade, Earnhardt had won three NASCAR Winston Cup championships, but he was still winless in the biggest race of them all — the Daytona 500.

As a result, the No. 1 question as the 1990 season began was, "When is Earnhardt going to win the Daytona 500?"

Earnhardt and his RCR crew thought this was finally going to be the year after

he rallied to win his 125-mile qualifying race in dramatic style. Despite being 12th with 10 laps to go, Earnhardt roared to the impressive victory.

And in the 500, Earnhardt led 26 of the first 27 laps and 155 in all including the white-flag lap. That's right — 155 of the 200.

But disaster struck on the final lap. Rick Wilson had suffered engine failure and a piece of metal from the bell housing had come to rest at the exit to turn two. Earnhardt didn't see it until it was too late as he ran over it and heard it hit the bottom of his car.

Immediately, the right rear tire went flat. Somehow Earnhardt kept his black Chevrolet off the wall, but his victory dreams were shattered as little-known Derrike Cope roared by to the shock of everyone — especially Earnhardt, his crew and wife Teresa watching on television in their motor home.

As a dejected and stunned Earnhardt sat in his car after limping back to the pits, he saw the CBS-TV crew heading his way. "I wanted to be anyplace else but there," said Earnhardt later. "But I told myself, 'You have to handle it just like Richard Petty would have done.'"

Earnhardt then told CBS's David Hobbs that "We ran over some debris and cut a right rear tire down, David, uh, just a quarter lap from victory."

That was not the last of Earnhardt's heartaches at Daytona. He had a chance to win the 500 again in 1991, '93, '95 and '96, but each time something or someone kept him from the winner's circle. Yet the despair of 1990 ranked as his toughest loss.

Most teams would have thrown the shredded tire away in frustration. Or burned it. Or cut it into little pieces and dropped them in a lake.

Instead, Earnhardt and Childress kept it as a daily reminder to never take anything for granted.

RACING against Dad

Dale Earnhardt admitted that one of the greatest joys of the 2000 NASCAR Winston Cup season was the chance to race against Dale Jr. on a weekly basis.

"I always wished I could have raced with my dad (Ralph)," said Earnhardt.

That only happened once.

Dale Sr. loved to tell that story. "One night in 1972 there was a Late Model Sportsman race at a track and the same night there was going to be a Grand National race (now called the Winston Cup Series) there," would begin Dale Sr.

"It was a pretty small field for the Grand National race so the (track) promoter said that the first six finishers in the Sportsman race also could run the Grand National, to fill out the field. I finished second, so I was added to the field.

"In the Grand National, I was running pretty good — fourth. My father was in the lead.

"I was trying to get by the guy who finished in front of me in the Sportsman race.

I was trying to get by the guy, but I just couldn't do it. He was faster.

"Well, as we come to the final lap, my father comes up behind me. He's just about lapped the field. He puts his bumper against mine and he starts pushing me! He pushes me right by that other guy, and I finished third.

"The other guy was so mad. He was screaming about the Earnhardts, but there was nothing he could do. It was a great feeling, that race. I never got to do it again before my dad died (in 1973)."

another kind of HORSEPOWER

As the train slowly crawled through the Alaska wilderness, a small house finally came into view. It was the first sign of civilization after seeing nothing in miles and miles of beautiful countryside.

And what is the first thing the people on the train saw as they passed by this home but a black No. 3 sign in the front window. "Even up here in the middle of nowhere he has his fans," said a passenger. "His fame is unbelievable."

There was no need to ask who he was. Even a nonracing fan knows what the black three signifies — Dale Earnhardt Sr.

Earnhardt is that well known. Even today, after his death, his fame and wealth continues to grow.

In a sport where having the most horsepower is a must if a race driver wants to win races, Earnhardt had even more horsepower off the track than his cars had on them.

During the late 1980s and 1990s, Earnhardt showed the world that a race car driver could earn much more money — a lot more — off the track than on.

The people at QVC still talk about the night that Earnhardt brought 13 items to the home-shopping network and in an hour, the entire warehouse was sold out. For a long time, it was QVC's busiest 60 minutes ever.

It was these kind of special off-track events that helped NASCAR Winston Cup racing attract a new and younger crowd and become the world's fastest-growing sport during the 1990s.

And one of the biggest reasons for the success of this type of specialty marketing was Earnhardt and his role as The Intimidator as he alone helped attract

Dale Earnhardt celebrates in victory lane after winning the 1980 National 500 at the Charlotte Motor Speedway.

many a new fan who wanted to see if the Man in Black lived up to his reputation.

And when they came to the race track, it was his souvenir trailer that they went to first.

Earnhardt lived up to that image even though he always said, "I never went into racing to be a bad guy, a good guy, any guy, just a good racer. I wanted to be Dale Earnhardt the racer.

"We've won races and championships not because I'm a good guy or bad guy. I'm a good racer. I've got a good race team and we are out there to win."

And he was a winner on and off the race track.

Earnhardt was a company in himself. At one time, he owned Sports Image, the biggest seller of merchandise in the racing world, most of it being Earnhardt's. And even after he sold the company,

Earnhardt owned the rights to everything dealing with his name.

Earnhardt also owned a huge farm in Iredell County, N.C., where he bred and raised registered Black Angus cattle and raised chickens for businessman Frank Perdue. Earnhardt was particularly proud of being a chicken farmer as he enjoyed talking about the four houses he had and the 7,500 eggs laid every day at each house.

Earnhardt acquired a moribund Chevrolet dealership in Newton, N.C., in the late1980s and turned it into a huge profit-maker.

As a driver, Earnhardt won more than $41 million. His souvenirs sold more than half of that on a yearly basis. And of course, that doesn't account for what he earned from his other businesses.

"He was a far more astute businessman than people realized," says Don

Hawk, who was Earnhardt's business manager through most of the 1990s. "He and (wife)Teresa were a heck of a team."

And today it is Teresa who is running Dale Earnhardt Inc.

Earnhardt's horsepower not only extended into the marketing and business world. He also was the main voice heard in the garage area when it came to various discussions with NASCAR. If a fellow competitor wanted to be heard, he knew the best way to do that was to ask Earnhardt to carry that idea forward.

Quite often if there was a dispute or controversy in the garage area, it was Earnhardt who quietly got the issue resolved — usually for the betterment of the sport.

In today's nomenclature, Earnhardt was "The Man" on and off the race track.

DEI: A
powerhouse team

Richard Petty has tried it. Bobby Allison has tried it. Cale Yarborough has tried it. Darrell Waltrip has tried it.

These are four of the greatest race car drivers in the history of NASCAR Winston Cup racing. Among the four of them they own 14 championships. Yet none of them has become a championship car owner. In fact, each one has struggled just to win more than a couple of races as a car owner.

In fact, when it comes to great race car drivers becoming great car owners, the list is quite short. You can count the number on one hand and have a couple of fingers left over. For a number of years, that list was confined to Lee Petty, and Junior Johnson and Lee had son Richard as his driver.

And that is why so many people were surprised by how successful Dale

Earnhardt was as a car owner. And what made Earnhardt's success even more amazing was he built this powerhouse of a team while still driving for a rival car owner.

Today, Dale Earnhardt Inc. (DEI) is regarded as one of the strongest teams on the Winston Cup Series. And the two people most responsible for this are Earnhardt and wife Teresa.

When DEI was first formed in 1985, it was strictly a way for Earnhardt to race on the NASCAR Busch Series. And with Earnhardt behind the wheel, it was a winning operation as he won 17 races in his own cars while running a limited schedule before deciding to retire from Busch Series at the end of 1994 season.

But instead of shutting down his race team, Earnhardt decided to expand his operation. First, he hired Jeff Green to run

Dale Earnhardt at Darlington in 1995.

the full Busch Series circuit beginning with the '95 season. Then, Earnhardt formed a NASCAR Craftsman Truck Series team with Ron Hornaday as the driver.

Hornaday brought DEI its first championship in 1996 by capturing the truck-series title. Hornaday won his second truck championship in '98.

Green finished in the top five in the Busch Series point race in both '95 and '96, but he failed to win a race in either season. So Earnhardt decided a change was needed and, to the surprise of many, named little-known Steve Park as his Busch Series driver.

And a few months later, Earnhardt pulled another surprise by saying DEI would expand its operation by running a team on the Winston Cup circuit with Park running five races in '97 and the full season in '98 with Pennzoil as the sponsor.

People immediately began to wonder who would drive the Busch Series car in 1998. The answer was Dale Earnhardt Jr.

Even Grandma wondered if Dale Jr. was ready. "I just thought he needed a lot more experience in the smaller divisions," said Martha Earnhardt. "But he proved me wrong."

That is quite an understatement as Dale Jr. gave DEI its third championship in his first full season on the Busch Series, winning seven races. And the young Earnhardt followed that up with another championship campaign in '99 as he won six more races.

It was during the 1998 season that Dale Sr. pulled off one of his biggest coups in his quest to make DEI a real powerhouse on the Winston Cup Series as he convinced Steve Hmiel to join his organization.

For 11 years Hmiel had been a main cog in Roush Racing and its rise to the top. But during the summer of '98, Hmiel left the team. Shortly afterward he received a call from Earnhardt.

"He said, 'Come down here and look at my race team,'" recalls Hmiel. "He

then added, 'I've called you a couple of times before, and you were loyal to Jack and I appreciate that. But now that you're not working (for him), would you come and work for me?'"

Hmiel agreed to come to the race shop and talk with Earnhardt. Once he did, he knew that "Dale wanted DEI to be the best. The facility had everything you need. Dale just felt he wanted a racer there every day to help it get to where he wanted."

After talking with Earnhardt, Hmiel jumped at the chance to help his former rival become a winning Winston Cup car owner.

And Hmiel, director of motor sports, along with Ty Norris, executive vice president of motor sports, have been the two main every-day players in helping DEI reach the goals set by Dale Sr.

During the '99 season, the elder Earnhardt announced that Dale Jr. would move up to the Winston Cup Series with

Budweiser as his sponsor.

Later that year Earnhardt said he was disbanding his truck-series team following the 1999 season with Hornaday replacing Dale Jr. as driver of the Busch Series car.

In his five seasons on the truck series, Hornaday won 25 races. That still is the most in the history of the series.

Before the start of the 2000 Winston Cup season, the elder Earnhardt said, "I couldn't be happier with the progress we are making at DEI. I think this is the year we get to victory lane."

And he was right with Dale Jr., appropriately, being the first DEI driver to win a Winston Cup event as he dominated the spring race at Texas. A month later, Dale Jr. won at Richmond. And this was followed by a victory in The Winston, NASCAR's all-star race.

Park also scored his first win during the 2000 season as he held off road racing expert Mark Martin at Watkins Glen, N.Y.

In September 2000, Earnhardt announced that he was adding a third Winston Cup team with Michael Waltrip as the driver and NAPA as the sponsor and he was closing down his Busch operation.

With the addition of the third team, the elder Earnhardt was convinced 2001 was going to be DEI's best season ever.

And he was even more sure of that as Earnhardt raced along in third place with Waltrip and Dale Jr. running one-two ahead of him as the 2001 Daytona 500 entered its final lap.

However, the elder Earnhardt never got to see his two cars cross the finish line running one-two with Waltrip scoring his first Winston Cup victory in the biggest race on the circuit as Dale Sr. was killed in a third-turn accident on the last lap.

DEI, led by Dale Jr.'s three wins, ended the 2001 season with five triumphs, cementing its place as one of the top teams on the circuit.

if God was a STOCK CAR DRIVER

During the last 15 years of Dale Earnhardt's racing career, the sign was seen more and more — "If God was a stock car driver, his name would be Earnhardt."

That is how his legions of fans saw the man known as The Intimidator. In their opinion, there has never been a better race car driver than Dale Earnhardt Sr.

And many others agree including Bill France Jr., the longtime president of NASCAR and now the chairman of NASCAR's board of directors, and Bud Moore, the longtime car owner who has been around the sport for more than 50 years.

In a statement released less than two hours after Earnhardt's death on the final lap of the 2001 Daytona 500, France said, "Today NASCAR lost its greatest driver in the history of the sport."

"You've got three kinds of drivers," said Moore on more than one occasion. "Over here is Earnhardt. Then you've got two or three others that can run with him. Then there's the rest of them."

After the first time Earnhardt was told what Moore had said, he admitted, "It's a hell of compliment coming from someone like Bud Moore.

"I'm just a guy from Kannapolis, N.C., a cotton-mill town, made it to the eighth grade in school. I went out there and did what I could do and excelled at what I could do."

Many times during his career Earnhardt was asked where he thought he ranked in a list of the sport's greatest drivers. "I haven't really thought about it," he would reply. "The only thing I worry about is winning ... races and the championship.

Special baseballs were made for the Kannapolis Intimidators with the number three.

"It's like hunting and fishing (his two favorite hobbies). You want to catch the most fish or shoot the most ducks — with the least shells. You don't want to be standing there with a whole pile of shells on the ground and one duck."

That never happened to the avid outdoorsman.

And when it came to the racing side of his life, the record books shows why so many people believe Earnhardt belongs at or near the top whenever the "who is the best driver" question is raised.

Only he and Richard Petty have won seven NASCAR Winston Cup championships. When Jeff Gordon won his fourth title in 2001, he moved into third place on this all-important list.

Earnhardt's 76 victories rank him sixth in the history of the sport. Petty, who stands first with 200 triumphs, wonders if Earnhardt's total might have been double if Earnhardt had raced during the 1960s when the series ran between 50

and 60 races a year and sometimes more. During most of Earnhardt's illustrious Winston Cup career which began in 1979, the number of races each year was between 29 and 32.

During the modern era (1972 on), only Darrell Waltrip won more races.

Earnhardt ranks third on the all-time superspeedway race winners list behind Petty and David Pearson with 48 triumphs, or the most during the modern era. Petty won 55 super speedway races, while Pearson won 49.

No driver has won more races at Daytona International Speedway than Earnhardt, who captured 34.

No driver has won more restrictor plate races than Earnhardt with 11.

In each case, the driver occupying the number two spot has less than half of Earnhardt's win total.

Earnhardt ranks first in the number of wins at Atlanta Motor Speedway with nine and Talladega Superspeedway with

10. He is second to David Pearson (10-9) in victories at Darlington. Earnhardt is tied for second on the all-time win list at Bristol (nine).

Only twice in 22 seasons of running the full circuit did Earnhardt finish out of the top 10 in the point race. And in 14 of those years, he ranked in the top five.

Between 1986 and 1995, Earnhardt won six championships and was second twice in the title chase.

He was selected the Driver of the Year five times by the National Motorsports Press Association. No other driver has won this award this many times including Richard Petty, for whom the award is named.

It would be hard to select any driver who drove harder or with more determination than Earnhardt.

And when all of this is added up it is not surprising why so many believe he deserves a spot at the very top of any listing of the greatest of them all.